낭독하는 명작동화

Level 3-4

# Pinocchio

✦· 피노키오 ·✦

새벽달(남수진) • 이현석 지음

## Key Vocabulary

명작동화를 읽기 전에 스토리의 **핵심 단어**를
확인해 보세요. 내가 알고 있는 단어라면 체크
표시하고, 모르는 단어는 이야기를 읽은 후에 체크
표시해 보세요.

## Story

Level 3의 영어 텍스트 수준은 책의 난이도를
측정하는 레벨 지수인 **AR(Accelerated
Reader) 지수 2.5~3.3 사이**로 **미국 초등
학생 2~3학년 수준**으로 맞추고, 분량을 **1100
단어 내외**로 구성했습니다.

쉬운 단어와 간결한 문장으로 구성된 스토리를
그림과 함께 읽어 보세요. 페이지마다 내용 이해를
돕는 그림이 있어 상상력을 풍부하게 해 주며,
이야기를 더욱 재미있게 읽을 수 있습니다.

## Reading Training

이현석 선생님의 **강세와 청킹 가이드**에 맞춰
명작동화를 낭독해 보세요.

한국어 번역으로 내용을 확인하고 **우리말 낭독**을
하는 것도 좋습니다.

# This Book

## Storytelling

명작동화의 내용을 떠올릴 수 있는 **8개의 그림**이 준비되어 있습니다. 각 그림당 제시된 **3개의 단어**를 활용하여 이야기를 만들고 말해 보세요. 상상력과 창의력을 기르는 데 큰 도움이 될 것입니다.

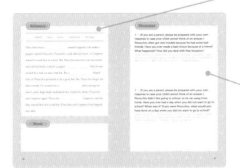

## Summary

명작동화의 **줄거리 요약문**이 제시되어 있습니다. 빈칸에 들어갈 단어를 채워 보며 이야기의 내용을 다시 정리해 보세요.

## Discussion

명작동화의 내용을 실생활에 응용하거나 비판적으로 생각해 볼 수 있는 **토론 질문**으로 구성했습니다. 영어 또는 우리말로 토론하며 책의 내용을 재구성해 보세요.

## 픽처 텔링 카드

특별부록으로 **16장의 이야기 그림 카드**가 맨 뒷장에 있어 한 장씩 뜯어서 활용이 가능합니다. 순서에 맞게 그림을 배열하고 이야기 말하기를 해 보세요.

QR코드 영상을 통해 새벽달님과 이현석 선생님이 이 책을 활용하는 가장 좋은 방법을 직접 설명해 드립니다!

# Contents

# Pinocchio

✦⊪• 피노키오 •⊪✦

# Key Vocabulary

- [ ] **carpenter** 목수
- [ ] **puppet** (인형극에 쓰는) 인형
- [ ] **carve** 조각하다, 깎아서 만들다
- [ ] **cricket** 귀뚜라미
- [ ] **chase away** 쫓아내다
- [ ] **plant** 심다
- [ ] **fairy** 요정
- [ ] **lie** 거짓말하다
- [ ] **carriage** 마차
- [ ] **donkey** 당나귀
- [ ] **fur** 털
- [ ] **tail** 꼬리
- [ ] **merchant** 상인
- [ ] **whale** 고래
- [ ] **swallow** 삼키다
- [ ] **raft** 뗏목
- [ ] **row** (배를) 젓다
- [ ] **shore** 해변

Once there was a kind carpenter named Geppetto.
He lived alone, so he wanted to have a son.

One day, Geppetto found some special wood.
'I will make a puppet with this wood,' he thought.
'It will look like a little boy.'

Geppetto took the wood home and sat at his desk.

He made a head and added two eyes.

The eyes moved and looked around.

"The eyes are moving!" said Geppetto.

Next, he carved a nose and a mouth.

Then the mouth began to talk.

"Hello, Geppetto!" it said.

"You can talk!" Geppetto was shocked but happy.

In the morning, Geppetto looked at the puppet.
"Your name is Pinocchio," he said.
"You are like my son."
The puppet could move its head, arms, and legs.

There was a cricket in the room.
He soon became Pinocchio's friend.

Geppetto wanted Pinocchio to go to school.
Geppetto was poor, so he only had one coat.
He sold it and bought a book for Pinocchio.

One day, Pinocchio wanted to see the world.

"I want to go outside," he said.

"The world is big, and you are small.

You have to go to school first," said Geppetto.

"No, I do not want to go to school!" said Pinocchio.

Then he burst open the door.

The cricket jumped up to Pinocchio's shoulder.

Then Pinocchio ran straight ahead.

"Pinocchio, come back!" Geppetto shouted.

Geppetto wanted to follow Pinocchio, but he was too slow.

The people on the street saw Pinocchio.

"Look! It is a running puppet!" they said.

Pinocchio smiled and waved at them.

Then, Pinocchio heard a sound at the end of the street.

The sound came from the puppet theater.

Pinocchio wanted to watch the show, but he had no money.

'I will sell my book and get some coins,' he thought.

"Pinocchio, the book is for your school.

Do not sell the book!" said the cricket.

Pinocchio did not like the cricket's words.

So he chased the cricket away.

Then, Pinocchio sold his book and bought the ticket.

He watched the show, and he danced, too.

The puppet master saw Pinocchio.
'He is a special puppet,' he thought.
He wanted Pinocchio for his show.

The puppet master took Pinocchio into his tent.
In the tent, Pinocchio saw the puppet master
hurting other puppets.
"I want to go home. Please let me go!" Pinocchio cried.
"My father sold his coat to buy me a book.
And I sold the book for your puppet show.
I want to go back and tell him I am sorry," he explained.

The puppet master felt bad for Pinocchio.
So he gave five gold coins to Pinocchio and let him go.

On the street, Pinocchio met a bad cat and a bad fox.

"Hello, little puppet," they said.

"We are your friends.

We know a secret magic field.

Plant your coins there, and you can get more gold."

Pinocchio was excited about the magic field.

He wanted to get more gold coins.

"Come with us," said the cat and the fox.

Pinocchio followed the bad cat and the bad fox.

They arrived at a town, and they were hungry.

So they went to a restaurant.

The cat and the fox ordered expensive food.
They ate a lot, and Pinocchio ate a little.
Then the cat and the fox left the restaurant.
They left without paying for the food.
So Pinocchio had to pay for everything.
He used four gold coins.
Pinocchio was sad and lonely.

But then, something magical happened.

A blue fairy appeared.

"Who are you?" Pinocchio asked.

"I am your fairy. I know everything about you," said the fairy.

Then she asked, "Where are your gold coins?"

"I do not have any," Pinocchio answered.

Suddenly, Pinocchio's nose grew longer.

His nose grew when he lied.

"Please help me," Pinocchio said to the fairy.

"My nose is strange."

"Okay, but you must listen to your father.

And you should go to school," said the fairy.

"I promise," said Pinocchio.

On the street, Pinocchio met the bad cat and the bad fox again.

They said, "Come with us to the magic field.

You need to plant your coin, right?"

Pinocchio nodded and followed them.

He forgot about the fairy's words.

Pinocchio arrived at the field.

There, he planted his last gold coin.

He waited for a gold coin tree to grow, but nothing happened.

Pinocchio started to cry.

He really wanted to go home.

Then the fairy came again and saved him.

Pinocchio promised to go back home and be a good boy.

The next day, Pinocchio was walking.

He met his friend on the street.

The friend told him about a magical place.

"I know a place called the Land of Toys," said the friend.

Then she asked, "Do you want to go there with me?

In that place, you can play all day. There is no school!"

"No school? Sure, I will go!" said Pinocchio.

Soon, a big carriage arrived in front of them.

Many donkeys were pulling the carriage.

Some donkeys were crying.

"Why are the donkeys crying?" Pinocchio asked the driver.

"Do not mind the donkeys," said the driver.

Pinocchio and his friend got into the carriage.

In the carriage, they saw young children smiling happily.

The carriage arrived in front of the Land of Toys.
Pinocchio and his friend went inside.
Children were running, laughing, and playing.
Pinocchio's eyes grew wide with wonder.

Pinocchio and his friend ran inside and played.
Night came, but the children did not stop playing.

Many days passed in the Land of Toys.
Pinocchio forgot about the fairy's words.
He forgot about Geppetto, too.

One night, Pinocchio's ears hurt very much.

He lifted his hands and touched his ears.

They were long, and they were covered with fur.

Pinocchio ran to a mirror and looked at them.

He was shocked because he had donkey ears!

Then Pinocchio's hips also hurt.

He turned his head and looked at them.

He had a donkey tail!

In the Land of Toys, children turned into donkeys
after playing too much and not going to school.
Then they were trained for circuses.
Pinocchio, now a donkey, went on the circus stage.
But he could not move well.
So, the circus owner sold Pinocchio to a merchant.

The merchant took Pinocchio to a ship to sell him away.
But he dropped Pinocchio into the sea by mistake.
Pinocchio turned back into a puppet in the water.
But suddenly, a big whale swallowed him.
And Pinocchio found Geppetto inside the whale's stomach!

There, Geppetto was on a raft.

"Geppetto, I missed you!" said Pinocchio.

Geppetto was happy to see his son.

Suddenly, the whale opened its mouth.

"Row the raft!" Pinocchio shouted.

Pinocchio and Geppetto rowed the raft out of the whale's mouth.

Finally, they were out on the shore.

On the shore, Pinocchio and Geppetto met the fairy.

"Well done, Pinocchio," said the fairy.

"You are a good boy because you saved Geppetto."

She waved her wand and turned Pinocchio
into a real human boy.

Since that day, Pinocchio went to school every day.

He no longer lied to anyone.

Pinocchio and Geppetto lived happily ever after.

### ◆ Pinocchio

**On**ce / there was a **kind car**penter / named Geppetto.
He **liv**ed al**o**ne, / so he **want**ed to **ha**ve a **son**.

**One** day, / Geppetto / **found** some **spe**cial **wood**.
'I will **ma**ke a **pup**pet / with this **wood**,' / he thought.
'It will **look** like / a **lit**tle **boy**.'

Geppetto **took** the **wood ho**me / and **sat** at his **desk**.
He **ma**de a **head** / and **add**ed **two e**yes.
The **e**yes **mo**ved / and **look**ed a**round**.
"The **e**yes are **mo**ving!" / said Geppetto.
**Next**, / he **car**ved a **no**se / and a **mouth**.
**Then** the **mouth** / be**gan** to **talk**.
"He**llo**, / Geppetto!" / it said.
"You can **talk**!" / Geppetto was **shock**ed / but **hap**py.

## ◆ 피노키오

옛날에 제페토라는 친절한 목수가 있었습니다.
그는 혼자 살았기 때문에 아들을 갖고 싶었어요.

어느 날, 제페토는 특별한 나무를 발견했습니다.
'이 나무로 인형을 만들어야겠어.' 제페토는 생각했습니다.
'꼬마 남자아이처럼 보이게 만들어야겠어.'

제페토는 그 나무를 집으로 가져와 작업대 앞에 앉았습니다.
그는 머리를 만들고 두 눈을 달았어요.
그 눈이 움직이며 주위를 둘러보았습니다.
"눈이 움직이고 있어!" 제페토가 말했어요.
다음으로, 제페토는 코와 입을 조각했습니다.
그러자 입이 말을 하기 시작했어요.
"안녕하세요, 제페토 아저씨!" 입이 말했습니다.
"너 말을 하는구나!" 제페토는 깜짝 놀랐지만 기뻤습니다.

In the **mor**ning, / Geppetto **look**ed at the **pup**pet.

"Your **na**me is Pi**no**cchio," / he said.

"You are like my **son**."

The **pup**pet / could **mo**ve its **head**, / **arms**, / and **legs**.


There was a **cri**cket / in the **room**.

He **soon** be**came** / Pinocchio's **fri**end.


Gep**pet**to **want**ed Pi**no**cchio / to **go** to **school**.

Gep**pet**to was **poor**, / so he **on**ly had **one coat**.

He **sold** it / and **bought** a **book** / for Pi**no**cchio.


**One** day, / Pi**no**cchio **want**ed to **see** the **world**.

"I **want** to go out**si**de," / he said.

"The **world** is **big**, / and you are **small**.

You **ha**ve to **go** to **school first**," / said Gep**pet**to.

아침이 되자, 제페토는 인형을 바라보았습니다.
"네 이름은 피노키오란다." 제페토가 말했어요.
"너는 내 아들 같구나."
인형은 머리, 팔, 그리고 다리를 움직일 수 있었습니다.

방 안에는 귀뚜라미 한 마리가 있었어요.
귀뚜라미는 곧 피노키오의 친구가 되었습니다.

제페토는 피노키오가 학교에 가기를 바랐습니다.
제페토는 가난했기 때문에 코트가 한 벌뿐이었어요.
그는 그 코트를 팔아서 피노키오에게 책을 사 주었습니다.

어느 날, 피노키오는 세상을 보고 싶었습니다.
"저는 밖으로 나가고 싶어요." 피노키오가 말했어요.
"세상은 크고, 너는 작단다.
너는 먼저 학교에 가야 해." 제페토가 말했습니다.

"No, **/** I do **not want** to go to **school**!" **/** said Pinocchio.

**Then /** he **burst o**pen the **door**.

The **crick**et **jump**ed **up /** to Pinocchio's **shou**lder.

**Then** Pinocchio **/** ran **straight** ahead.

"Pinocchio, **/** come **back**!" **/** Gep**pet**to **shout**ed.

Gep**pet**to **want**ed to **fol**low Pinocchio, **/** but he was **too slow**.


The **peo**ple on the **street /** saw Pinocchio.

"**Look**! **/** It is a **run**ning **pup**pet!" **/** they said.

Pinocchio **smil**ed **/** and **wav**ed at them.


**Then**, **/** Pinocchio **heard** a **sound /** at the **end** of the **street**.

The **sound ca**me **/** from the **pup**pet **the**ater.

Pinocchio **/ want**ed to **watch** the **show**, **/** but he had **no mo**ney.

'I will **sell** my **book /** and **get** some **coins**,' **/** he thought.

"Pinocchio, **/** the **book** is for your **school**.

Do **not sell** the **book**!" **/** said the **crick**et.

Pinocchio did **not li**ke **/** the **crick**et's **words**.

So he **cha**sed the **crick**et a**way**.

**Then**, **/** Pinocchio **sold** his **book /** and **bought** the **tic**ket.

He **watch**ed the **show**, **/** and he **dan**ced, too.

"싫어요, 저는 학교 가기 싫어요!" 피노키오가 말했습니다.

그러고 나서 그는 문을 벌컥 열었어요.

귀뚜라미가 피노키오의 어깨 위로 뛰어올랐습니다.

그러자 피노키오는 곧장 앞으로 달려 나갔어요.

"피노키오, 돌아와!" 제페토가 외쳤습니다.

제페토는 피노키오를 따라가고 싶었지만, 너무 느렸어요.


거리의 사람들이 피노키오를 보았습니다.

"봐! 달리는 인형이야!" 사람들이 말했어요.

피노키오는 웃으며 사람들에게 손을 흔들었습니다.


그때, 피노키오는 거리 끝에서 어떤 소리를 들었습니다.

그 소리는 인형 극장에서 흘러나오고 있었어요.

피노키오는 인형극을 보고 싶었지만, 그에게는 돈이 없었습니다.

'책을 팔아서 돈을 좀 마련해야겠어.' 피노키오가 생각했어요.

"피노키오, 그 책은 학교 갈 때 필요한 거잖아.

그 책을 팔지 마!" 귀뚜라미가 말했습니다.

피노키오는 귀뚜라미의 말을 마음에 들어 하지 않았어요.

그래서 그는 귀뚜라미를 쫓아냈어요.

그러고 나서, 피노키오는 책을 팔아 표를 샀어요.

그는 인형극을 구경했고, 춤도 추었습니다.

The **pup**pet **mas**ter / **saw** Pino**cc**hio.

'He is a **spe**cial **pup**pet,' / he thought.

He **want**ed Pino**cc**hio / for his **show**.


The **pup**pet **mas**ter / **took** Pino**cc**hio into his **tent**.

In the **tent**, / Pino**cc**hio **saw** the **pup**pet **mas**ter / **hurt**ing other **pup**pets.

"I **want** to go **ho**me. / **Plea**se **let** me **go**!" / Pino**cc**hio cried.

"My **fa**ther **sold** his **coat** / to **buy** me a **book**.

And I **sold** the **book** / for your **pup**pet **show**.

I **want** to **go** back and **tell** him / I am **sor**ry," / he explained.


The **pup**pet **mas**ter felt **bad** / for Pino**cc**hio.

So he **ga**ve **fi**ve gold **coins** to Pino**cc**hio / and **let** him **go**.


On the **street**, / Pino**cc**hio met a **bad cat** / and a **bad fox**.

"He**llo**, **lit**tle **pup**pet," / they said.

"**We** are your **fri**ends. / We **know** a **se**cret **ma**gic **field**.

**Plant** your **coins** there, / and you can **get** more **gold**."

Pino**cc**hio was ex**ci**ted / about the **ma**gic **field**.

He **want**ed to **get** / **mo**re gold **coins**.

"**Co**me with **us**," / said the **cat** and the **fox**.

32

인형극단의 단장이 피노키오를 보았습니다.

'저 아이는 특별한 인형이로군.' 단장이 생각했어요.

단장은 자신의 인형극에 피노키오를 쓰고 싶었습니다.


인형극단의 단장은 피노키오를 자신의 천막 안으로 데려갔습니다.

텐트 안에서, 피노키오는 단장이 다른 인형들을 괴롭히는 것을 보았어요.

"저 집에 가고 싶어요. 제발 보내 주세요!" 피노키오가 울면서 말했습니다.

"제 아버지는 저에게 책을 사 주시기 위해 코트를 파셨어요.

그리고 저는 그 책을 팔아서 단장님의 인형극을 본 거고요.

돌아가서 아버지에게 죄송하다고 말씀드리고 싶어요." 피노키오가 설명했어요.


인형극단의 단장은 피노키오를 안쓰럽게 여겼어요.

그래서 그는 피노키오에게 금화 다섯 닢을 주면서 보내 주었어요.


길에서, 피노키오는 나쁜 고양이와 나쁜 여우를 만났습니다.

"안녕, 꼬마 인형." 그들이 말했어요.

"우리는 너의 친구야. 우리는 아무도 모르는 마법의 밭을 알아.

그곳에 동전을 심으면, 너는 더 많은 금을 얻을 수 있어."

피노키오는 마법의 밭 생각에 신이 났습니다.

그는 더 많은 금화를 얻고 싶었어요.

"우리와 함께 가자." 고양이와 여우가 말했습니다.

Pinocchio / followed the **bad cat** / and the **bad fox**.

They arrived at a **town**, / and they were **hun**gry.

So they **went** to a **rest**aurant.


The **cat** and the **fox** / ordered expensive **food**.

They **ate** a **lot**, / and Pinocchio **ate** a **lit**tle.

**Then** the **cat** and the **fox** / **left** the **rest**aurant.

They **left** / without **pay**ing for the **food**.

So Pinocchio / had to **pay** for everything.

He used **four** gold **coins**.

Pinocchio / was **sad** and **lone**ly.


But **then**, / something **mag**ical **hap**pened.

A **blue fair**y appeared.

"Who **are** you?" / Pinocchio asked.

"I am your **fair**y. / I **know** everything about you," / said the **fair**y.

**Then** she asked, / "**Where** are your **gold coins**?"

"I do **not ha**ve any," / Pinocchio answered.


**Sud**denly, / Pinocchio's **nose** / **grew long**er.

His **no**se **grew** / when he **lied**.

"**Plea**se **help** me," / Pinocchio said to the **fair**y.

"My **no**se is **stran**ge."

"O**kay**, / but you **must lis**ten / to your **fa**ther.

And you should **go** to **school**," / said the **fair**y.

"I **pro**mise," / said Pinocchio.

피노키오는 나쁜 고양이와 나쁜 여우를 따라갔습니다.
그들은 한 마을에 도착했고, 배가 고팠어요.
그래서 그들은 식당에 갔습니다.

고양이와 여우는 비싼 음식을 주문했습니다.
그들은 많이 먹었고, 피노키오는 조금만 먹었어요.
그리고 나서 고양이와 여우는 식당을 떠났습니다.
그들은 음식값을 내지 않고 가 버렸어요.
그래서 피노키오가 모든 비용을 지불해야 했습니다.
그는 금화 네 닢을 지불했어요.
피노키오는 슬프고 외로웠습니다.

하지만 그때, 마법 같은 일이 일어났습니다.
푸른 요정이 나타난 거예요.
"당신은 누구세요?" 피노키오가 물었습니다.
"나는 너의 요정이야. 나는 너에 대한 모든 것을 알고 있지." 요정이 말했어요.
이어서 요정이 물었습니다. "네 금화는 어디 있지?"
"저는 금화가 하나도 없어요." 피노키오가 대답했어요.

갑자기, 피노키오의 코가 길어졌습니다.
거짓말을 할 때마다 피노키오의 코는 길어졌어요.
"부디 저를 도와주세요." 피노키오가 요정에게 말했습니다.
"제 코가 이상해요."
"좋아, 하지만 너는 네 아버지 말씀을 잘 들어야 해.
그리고 너는 학교에 가야 해." 요정이 말했어요.
"약속할게요." 피노키오가 말했습니다.

On the **street**, **/** Pinocchio **/** **met** the **bad cat** and the **bad fox** again.

They said, **/** "**Co**me with **us /** to the **ma**gic **field**.

You **need** to **plant** your **coin**, **/** **right**?"

Pi**no**cchio **nod**ded **/** and **fol**lowed them.

He for**got** about the **fair**y's **words**.


Pi**no**cchio ar**ri**ved **/** at the **field**.

**There**, **/** he **plant**ed his **last gold coin**.

He **wait**ed for a **gold coin tree** to **grow**, **/** but **no**thing **ha**ppened.


Pi**no**cchio **start**ed to **cry**.

He **real**ly **/** **want**ed to **go ho**me.

**Then** the **fair**y **ca**me a**gain /** and **sa**ved him.

Pi**no**cchio **pro**mised to **go** back **ho**me **/** and **be** a **good boy**.


The **next** day, **/** Pi**no**cchio was **walk**ing.

He **met** his **fri**end **/** on the **street**.

The **fri**end **told** him **/** about a **ma**gical **pla**ce.

"I **know** a **pla**ce **/** **call**ed the **Land** of **Toys**," **/** said the **fri**end.

**Then** she asked, **/** "Do you **want** to **go** there with me?

In **that pla**ce, **/** you can **play all** day. **/** There is **no school**!"

"**No school**? **/** **Su**re, I will **go**!" **/** said Pi**no**cchio.

길에서, 피노키오는 나쁜 고양이와 나쁜 여우를 다시 만났습니다.
그들이 말했습니다. "우리와 함께 마법의 밭으로 가자.
너 동전 심어야지, 안 그래?"
피노키오는 고개를 끄덕이고 그들을 따라갔습니다.
그는 요정이 한 말을 잊어버렸어요.

피노키오는 밭에 도착했어요.
그곳에서 피노키오는 자신의 마지막 금화를 심었습니다.
그는 금화 나무가 자라기를 기다렸지만, 아무 일도 일어나지 않았어요.

피노키오는 울기 시작했어요.
그는 정말로 집에 가고 싶었습니다.
그러자 요정이 다시 찾아와서 그를 구해 주었어요.
피노키오는 집으로 돌아가서 착한 소년이 되겠다고 약속했습니다.

다음 날, 피노키오는 길을 걷고 있었습니다.
그는 길에서 친구를 만났어요.
그 친구가 피노키오에게 마법의 장소에 대해 말해 주었습니다.
"나는 장난감 나라라는 곳을 알아." 친구가 말했어요.
친구는 이어서 물었습니다. "너 나랑 그곳에 갈래?
거기서는 하루 종일 놀 수 있어. 그곳에는 학교도 없어!"
"학교가 없다고? 당연히 갈래!" 피노키오가 말했어요.

**Soon**, / a **big car**riage ar**ri**ved / in **front** of them.

**Ma**ny **don**keys / were **pull**ing the **car**riage.

**So**me **don**keys / were **cry**ing.

"**Why** are the **don**keys **cry**ing?" / Pi**no**cchio asked the **dri**ver.

"Do **not mind** the **don**keys," / said the **dri**ver.

Pi**no**cchio and his **fri**end / **got** into the **car**riage.

In the **car**riage, / they **saw young child**ren / **smi**ling **hap**pily.


The **car**riage ar**ri**ved / in **front** of the **Land** of **Toys**.

Pi**no**cchio and his **fri**end / went in**si**de.

**Child**ren were **run**ning, / **laugh**ing, / and **play**ing.

Pi**no**cchio's **e**yes / grew **wi**de with **won**der.


Pi**no**cchio and his **fri**end / **ran** in**si**de and **play**ed.

**Night** came, / but the **child**ren / did **not stop play**ing.


**Ma**ny days **pass**ed / in the **Land** of **Toys**.

Pi**no**cchio / for**got** about the **fair**y's **words**.

He for**got** about Gep**pet**to, **too**.

곧, 커다란 마차가 그들 앞에 도착했습니다.
많은 당나귀들이 그 마차를 끌고 있었어요.
몇몇 당나귀들은 울고 있었습니다.
"저 당나귀들이 왜 울고 있죠?" 피노키오가 마부에게 물었습니다.
"당나귀들은 신경 쓰지 마." 마부가 말했어요.
피노키오와 친구는 마차에 탔습니다.
마차에서 그들은 어린아이들이 행복하게 웃고 있는 모습을 보았어요.

마차는 장난감 나라 앞에 도착했습니다.
피노키오와 친구는 안으로 들어갔어요.
아이들이 뛰어다니며, 웃고, 놀고 있었습니다.
피노키오의 두 눈은 놀라움으로 커졌어요.

피노키오와 친구는 안으로 달려가 놀았습니다.
밤이 되었지만, 아이들은 노는 것을 멈추지 않았어요.

장난감 나라에서 많은 날들이 지났습니다.
피노키오는 요정이 한 말을 잊고 말았어요.
그는 제페토도 잊어버렸어요.

One night, / Pinocchio's ears / hurt very much.
He lifted his hands / and touched his ears.
They were long, / and they were covered with fur.
Pinocchio ran to a mirror / and looked at them.
He was shocked / because he had donkey ears!
Then / Pinocchio's hips also hurt.
He turned his head / and looked at them.
He had a donkey tail!

In the Land of Toys, / children turned into donkeys /
after playing too much / and not going to school.
Then they were trained / for circuses.
Pinocchio, / now a donkey, / went on the circus stage.
But he could not move well.
So, the circus owner / sold Pinocchio to a merchant.

The merchant / took Pinocchio to a ship / to sell him away.
But he dropped Pinocchio / into the sea by mistake.
Pinocchio turned back into a puppet / in the water.
But suddenly, / a big whale / swallowed him.
And Pinocchio found Geppetto / inside the whale's stomach!

어느 날 밤, 피노키오는 귀가 매우 아팠습니다.

그는 손을 들어서 귀를 만져 보았어요.

귀가 길어졌고 털로 덮여 있었습니다.

피노키오는 거울로 달려가서 귀를 봤어요.

그는 자신에게 당나귀 귀가 달린 것을 보고 깜짝 놀랐어요!

그때 피노키오의 엉덩이도 아파 왔습니다.

그는 고개를 돌려서 엉덩이를 보았습니다.

당나귀 꼬리까지 생긴 거예요!


장난감 나라에서, 아이들은 너무 많이 놀고

학교에 가지 않으면 당나귀로 변했습니다.

그리고 나서 그들은 서커스 훈련을 받았어요.

이제 당나귀가 된 피노키오도, 서커스 무대에 올랐습니다.

하지만 그는 잘 움직이지 못했어요.

그래서, 서커스 단장은 피노키오를 한 상인에게 팔아 버렸어요.


상인은 피노키오를 팔아 버리기 위해 배에 태웠습니다.

하지만 실수로 피노키오를 바다에 빠뜨리고 말았어요.

물속에서 피노키오는 다시 인형으로 변했습니다.

그런데 갑자기, 커다란 고래가 피노키오를 삼켰어요.

그리고 피노키오는 고래의 배 속에서 제페토를 만났어요!

## Reading Training

**There**, Geppetto **/** was on a **raft**.

"Geppetto, I **miss**ed you!" **/** said Pinocchio.

Geppetto was **hap**py **/** to **see** his **son**.

**Sud**denly, **/** the **wha**le **o**pened its **mouth**.

"**Row** the **raft**!" **/** Pinocchio **shout**ed.

Pinocchio and Gep**pet**to **/** **row**ed the **raft** **/** **out** of the **wha**le's **mouth**.

**Fin**ally, **/** they were **out** **/** on the **sho**re.


On the **sho**re, **/** Pinocchio and Gep**pet**to **met** the **fair**y.

"**Well** done, Pi**no**cchio," **/** said the **fair**y.

"You are a **good boy** **/** because you **sa**ved Gep**pet**to."

She **wa**ved her **wand** **/** and **turn**ed Pi**no**cchio **/** into a **real** human **boy**.


**Sin**ce that **day**, **/** Pinocchio **went** to **school** **/** every **day**.

He **no long**er **/** **li**ed to **any**one.

Pi**no**cchio and Gep**pet**to **/** **li**ved **hap**pily ever **af**ter.

그곳에서, 제페토는 뗏목을 타고 있었습니다.
"제페토 아저씨, 보고 싶었어요!" 피노키오가 말했어요.
제페토는 아들을 보아서 매우 기뻤습니다.
갑자기, 고래가 입을 벌렸습니다.
"뗏목을 저으세요!" 피노키오가 외쳤어요.
피노키오와 제페토는 뗏목을 저어 고래 입 밖으로 나왔어요.
마침내, 그들은 해변에 도착했어요.

해변에서, 피노키오와 제페토는 요정을 만났습니다.
"잘했어, 피노키오." 요정이 말했어요.
"제페토 아저씨를 구했으니 너는 착한 아이로구나."
요정은 마법 지팡이를 흔들었고 피노키오를 진짜 인간 남자아이로 바꿔 놓았습니다.

그날부터, 피노키오는 매일 학교에 갔습니다.
그는 더 이상 아무에게도 거짓말하지 않았어요.
피노키오와 제페토는 오래오래 행복하게 살았답니다.

## Part 1 ◆ p.8~15

Geppetto, wood, carve

world, cricket, run

master, tent, coins

friend, field, restaurant

fairy, nose, lie

carriage, play, forget

ears, donkey, tail

whale, raft, shore

## Summary

saved    fairy    show    carpenter    donkey

Once there was a _____ named Geppetto. He made a puppet named Pinocchio. Pinocchio could talk and move, so Geppetto wanted to send him to school. But Pinocchio wanted to see the world, and sold his book to watch a puppet _____. Then he was tricked by a bad cat and a bad fox. But a _____ helped him, so Pinocchio promised to be a good boy. But Pinocchio forgot the fairy's words. He turned into a _____ after playing too much, and a large whale swallowed him. Inside the whale, Pinocchio met Geppetto again. Pinocchio _____ Geppetto, and the fairy turned him into a real boy. Pinocchio and Geppetto lived happily ever after.

## Memo

**1** ◆ (If you are a parent, please be prepared with your own response in case your child cannot think of an answer.) Pinocchio often got into trouble because he had some bad friends. Have you ever made a bad choice because of a friend? What happened? How did you deal with that situation?

(여러분이 부모라면, 아이가 대답을 생각하지 못할 수 있으니 여러분의 경험을 미리 생각해 두었다가 들려주세요.) 피노키오는 나쁜 친구들과 어울리다가 곤경에 빠지고는 했어요. 여러분도 혹시 친구 때문에 잘못된 선택을 한 적이 있나요? 구체적으로 어떤 일이 있었나요? 그리고 그 상황을 어떻게 해결했나요?

**2** ◆ (If you are a parent, please be prepared with your own response in case your child cannot think of an answer.) Pinocchio didn't like going to school, so he ran away from home. Have you ever had a day when you did not want to go to school? When was it? If you were Pinocchio, what would you have done on a day when you did not want to go to school?

(여러분이 부모라면, 아이가 대답을 생각하지 못할 수 있으니 여러분의 경험을 미리 생각해 두었다가 들려주세요.) 피노키오는 학교 가는 것이 싫어서 가출까지 합니다. 여러분도 학교에 가기 싫은 날이 있었나요? 언제였나요? 여러분이 피노키오였다면 학교에 가기 싫은 날에 어떻게 했을까요?

낭독하는 명작동화 Level 3-4
Pinocchio

**초판 1쇄 발행** 2024년 12월 2일

**지은이** 새벽달(남수진)  이현석  롱테일 교육 연구소
**책임편집** 강지희 | **편집** 명채린  백지연  홍하늘
**디자인** 박새롬 | **그림** 김주연
**마케팅** 두잉글 사업본부

**펴낸이** 이수영
**펴낸곳** 롱테일북스
**출판등록** 제2015-000191호
**주소** 04033 서울특별시 마포구 양화로 113, 3층(서교동, 순흥빌딩)
**전자메일** team@ltinc.net

이 도서는 대한민국에서 제작되었습니다.
롱테일북스는 롱테일㈜의 출판 브랜드입니다.

ISBN  979-11-93992-28-9  14740

Pinocchio

**2**

puppet
cricket
book

새벽달 X 이현석 낭독스쿨

Pinocchio

**1**

wood
carve
talk

새벽달 X 이현석 낭독스쿨

Pinocchio

**4**

theater
show
sell

새벽달 X 이현석 낭독스쿨

Pinocchio

**3**

world
shoulder
run

새벽달 X 이현석 낭독스쿨

Pinocchio

**6**

field
plant
follow

새벽달 X 이현석 낭독스쿨

Pinocchio

**5**

master
cry
coins

새벽달 X 이현석 낭독스쿨

Pinocchio

**8**

fairy
nose
listen to

새벽달 X 이현석 낭독스쿨

Pinocchio

**7**

expensive
leave
pay

새벽달 X 이현석 낭독스쿨